THE FIELD GUIDE TO
WHITE
PEOPLE

D0018845

Copyright © 2000 by Stephan Dweck and Monteria Ivey

All rights reserved. No part of this book may be reproduced or
transmitted in any form or by any means, electronic or
mechanical, including photocopying, recording, or by any
information storage and retrieval system, without permission in
writing from the publisher.

Published by Three Rivers Press, 201 East 50th Street, New York,
New York 10022. Member of the Crown Publishing Group.

Random House, Inc. New York, Toronto, London, Sydney,
Auckland
www.randomhouse.com

THREE RIVERS PRESS is a registered trademark of Random
House, Inc.

Printed in the United States of America

Book design by Leonard Henderson

Library of Congress Cataloging-in-Publication Data

ISBN 0-609-80542-8

10   9   8   7   6   5   4   3   2   1

First Edition

THE FIELD GUIDE TO
WHITE
PEOPLE

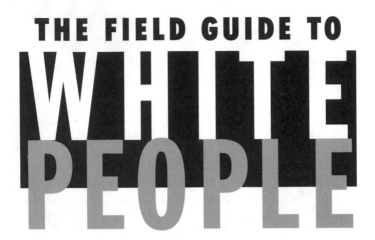

STEPHAN DWECK AND MONTERIA IVEY

THREE RIVERS PRESS

NEW YORK

"To the men in my family, Abe Dweck and Mitchell Menefee, who always had a laugh and a smile; and to Elan, Kimberly, Eve Marie, and Vaughn, Jr., who will carry the humor into the 21st Century.   —Stephan Dweck

"To my family, for their continued support; and the staff and assorted characters at Starbucks on 102nd Street and Broadway in New York City. Thanks for all the creative inspiration, ice water, and frappuccinos."

—Monteria Ivey

CONTENTS

ACKNOWLEDGMENTS

We would like to thank the following people for their support, love, and guidance: Lisa Jones, Ayesha Pande, Ray Murphy, Gary Sharffin, Nancy Yost, Barbara Lowenstein, Jason Spitz, David Colden, Sandy Epstein, the Endeavor Agency, Don Imus, Chris Rock, Will Schwalbe, the Dweck family, the Ivey family, Larry Dais, Chester Mapp, Kendall Minter, Dedra Tate, Jeanine Tate, Bob Tate, Tracia Decambre, Karen & Howard Baldwin, Adrienne Lopez, Gayle King, David Millstone, Craig "The Fig-Man" Figuerido, JoJo Archer, Claude Ismael, the temp "slaves" at Millberg & Weiss, Lawrence Hilton-Jacobs, Carey "The Wolf Man" Thomas, Bob Weiss, Yelda Tehranian, Yvette Coit, Arlene Levine, Sharon Parker, Bart Bartelamayo, Bernard McGirt, Charles McCord, Cheryl Abbott, Eddie "Coco" Green, Carol Greene, Bob, Lynn, RJ, and Mike Lucas, Mike Sargent, Alice Norris, Jody Milano, the Douglas Crew, Tina Douglas, Debbie Washington, Hazel Estwick, Donna Campbell, Jeanine DuBison, Alicia-Jordan Abbey, Bob "Spiceman" Fredericks, and all the white people we ever worked with, threatened, or met at Starbucks.

INTRODUCTION

Welcome to *The Field Guide to White People*—the authentic, must have, absolutely essential guide to understanding white people.

We admit that's a bold proclamation. But as we enter a new millennium there is a need for a guide to help us close the chasm that is the great racial divide in our country. The world moves at a breakneck pace, which means that people need a resource that can quickly and easily provide the means to eliminate long-held stereotypical beliefs. This guide (along with the forthcoming companion, *Field Guide to Black People*) is designed to put you on the road to true racial harmony and to make it possible for us all to "just get along."

How can we make such a claim? Easy. We're humorists, and this book is a parody. We have all seen how ignorance and prejudice have created a cultural divide within our society (in a perfect world Louis Farrakhan and Strom Thurmond would be fishing buddies). Why a field guide? Because no one is born with prejudice or racism. But somewhere along the way we pick up false notions, and like a bad habit, we just can't shake them until life gives us a crash course in reality. The first step to peace and harmony is understanding. You can't understand what you don't really know. That's where we come in. Here, in one handy package, we've combined years of field research with our in-depth anthropological knowledge to offer a guide to all the main species of white people.

The biggest mistake we make is to lump all white people into one homogeneous collective. Nothing could be further from the truth. White people of the continental United States are a diverse and fascinating group. To this end the *Field Guide* tries to capture as many varied types of white people as possible. Nevertheless, the spectrum of white people is too vast to capture in a single volume. Therefore it is possible that you will come across descriptions of white people previously unfamiliar to you and not see some of the more common members of the species you're used to encountering in your daily life.

The *Field Guide* separates white people into categories, or species (*Bible Thumpers, Georgia Peaches, Trailer Trash,* etc.). When you see a white person in the field, there are several ways you can use this guide to determine his or her identity. For each species we provide the following information:

Illustration of a typical member of the breed

Recognizable Traits

Similar Species

Range

Natural Habitat

Mating Behavior

Child Rearing Habits

Vacation Spots

Favorite Movies

Favorite Television Shows

Things You Find in Their Home

Survival Tips

Not all species of white people are open and receptive to outside contact. Hence, we provide *survival tips*—precautionary measures to handle hostile environments and chance encounters (wrestling matches, Klan meetings, steam baths with Bob Dole, etc.).

Searching for white people often involves *looking for evidence that white people have been present in an environment* rather than actually *seeing* white people. For example, if you board a train and notice a pamphlet from the John Birch Society on the vacated seat, odds are a white person was there before you. Lastly, to actually observe white people in their natural habitat(s) requires patience, alertness, and a keen understanding. With the help of this field guide we have no doubt that anyone can examine and enjoy the study of white people without risking embarrassment, affirmative action backlash, or police brutality.

Good luck.

THE FIELD GUIDE TO
WHITE
PEOPLE

The motto most appropriate for this species is: *"Behind every great sin is somebody holding a Bible."* Greed, avarice, lust, adultery, fornication, abuse, high cholesterol . . . no one in North America gets more frequent redemption miles than this species. The only thing more astounding than the breadth of their moral transgressions is their ability to turn public humiliation into a call for spiritual fundraising. Leather-bound Bibles (autographed by Jesus), Last Supper cookbooks (the specialty is the "Judas Salad" with a touch of hemlock), and Disciple Diapers are just a few of the items that can be found at their religious novelty shops. The only hymn in their songbook is *"Send in the money . . . for Jesus . . . "*

RECOGNIZABLE TRAITS

Bible prayer cloth, ten-dollar whores in need of "spiritual comforting," and hundreds of receipts from contributions to the 700 Club. Females of this species are distinguished by thick layers of cheap makeup in garish colors.

SIMILAR SPECIES

The Southern (Hick) Farmer

Distinguished from the Bible Thumper by the red-leather raw neck, pick-up truck, and Confederate underwear. See more details about this species on page 82.

RANGE

Southeastern United States. They have also been sighted in the American Southwest and at numerous Cadillac dealerships across the country.

NATURAL HABITAT

Baptist churches, WWF wrestling matches, demolition derbys, high school football games, and any Hooters that doesn't close on Sundays.

MATING BEHAVIOR

Has problem with copulation due to poor blood circulation. However, penis usually functions when he sings "Swing low, sweet chariot . . ." Mating period is very specific: occurs before and after menstruation (only "Demons" do it during) and only between Good Friday and Easter.

CHILD REARING HABITS

Baby's first gift is a G.I. Jesus. Makes children attend school on Martin Luther King Jr. Day. Refuses to give child Hostess cupcakes because they are made with

devil's food cake.

VACATION SPOTS

Everyone's front door on Saturday morning (to recruit converts)

Grand Ole Opry

Graceland

Dollyland (Dolly's bra size confirms that there is a God)

FAVORITE MOVIES

The Ten Commandments

The Robe

Gone With the Wind

Porno movies on Spectra Vision

FAVORITE TELEVISION SHOWS

Reruns of Petticoat Junction *(the only thing black in Hooterville was the little train rolling down the track)*

The Gospel according to Jimmy Swaggert

Baywatch

THINGS YOU FIND IN THEIR HOME

Gold-plated Bible autographed by Billy Graham

Sin-Soap, "to wash away temptation"

A new pair of Air Jordan's for walking on water

SURVIVAL TIPS

If you find yourself outnumbered by this species, always advocate "the father, the ghost, and the holy bombing of abortion clinics."

At PTA meetings, support school prayer, bring angel food cake to bake sales, and never refer to Ronald Reagan as "the devil's son."

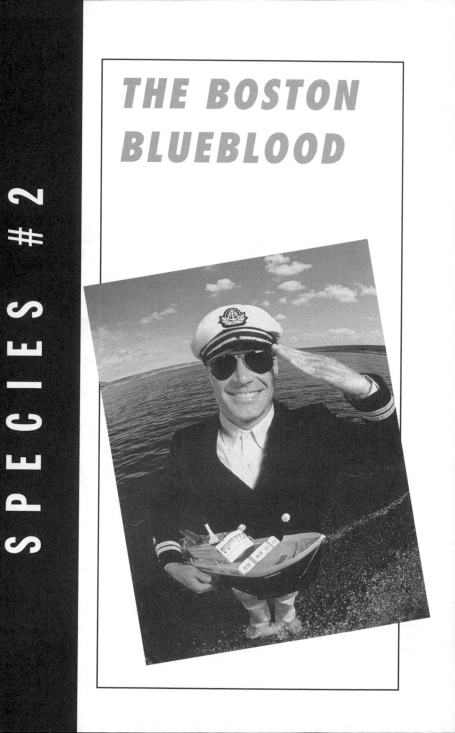

This species takes great pride in the fact that their ancestors were among the first thieves, rapists, and social outcasts to arrive on the shores of the great "new world" called America. Prominent Bluebloods played major roles in the American Revolution, the Civil War, and the Salem witch hunts. Thanks to genetics, today's Bluebloods need no aid in being able to walk in a manner befitting someone who has a pole stuck up their ass. Their credo is borrowed from the Kennedy clan: *"You're either with us . . . or we drown you!"*

RECOGNIZABLE TRAITS

Smoking pipe, monogrammed shirt and jacket, Burberry trenchcoat, L.L. Bean shoes, and handkerchief containing stains of bean and cod. The females can be identified by their Jackie Kennedy Onassis haircut, Queen Victoria bras (for the upright nipple), and a week's supply of diet pills.

SIMILAR SPECIES

The Connecticut Yankee

Usually poorer, self-sufficient, and leading a
rural existence. High rate of alcoholism and
incest. Look for in-laws that
have the same parents.

The Virginia Squire

Similar traits and Revolutionary heritage as a
Boston Blueblood, but distinguished by
slave/plantation legacy.

RANGE

Fairly common throughout New England but
has now extended its range to the entire
United States.

NATURAL HABITAT

Protestant churches, Bostonian private clubs,
polo fields, universities that cost more
than $30,000 per year with a college
motto in Latin, and any lecture by
William F. Buckley Jr.

MATING BEHAVIOR

Due to their Puritan ethics, they always make
love with the lights on (missionary position
only), next to a copy of *Paradise Lost*.

CHILD REARING HABITS

Children must use pacifier and stay in stroller until twelve years old. No spankings unless signed off by "Mummy and Daddy's" therapist. Children can only eat meals made with mayonnaise from the *WASP Cookbook*.

VACATION SPOTS

Killington, Vermont (winter)

Cape Cod (summer)

FAVORITE MOVIES

On Golden Pond

Love Story

Any film where the British win and the women are not frigid

FAVORITE TELEVISION SHOWS

None (they're still waiting for the
return of Peyton Place*)*

THINGS YOU FIND IN THEIR HOME

Antique furniture

Pilgrim Barneys

Three-month supply of New England clam
chowder

Nude pictures of historian Doris Kearns Goodwin

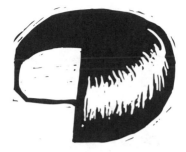

SURVIVAL TIPS

Always refer to a large sandwich as a grinder.
Remember, to many of these people Hal-
loween is a religious holiday. Never . . .
ever . . . ever . . . mention New York City or
Bucky Dent.

SPECIES # 3

THE
WEEKEND
WARRIOR

STATE

7

Without this species (along with their willing families) the American economy would go the way of the Roman Empire. This species, often referred to as "the working stiff," is responsible for the mass consumption of beer, potato chips, fast food, TV dinners, frozen pizza, chicken nuggets, and deodorant "that's strong enough for a man, but made for a woman." These failed athletes have a devotion to sport that borders on maniacal. The interesting paradox is that without the presence of this species there would be no multimillion-dollar contracts, state-of-the-art stadiums, or ESPN 2. Years of soft living have resulted in a biological attachment to their E-Z Boy recliners.

RECOGNIZABLE TRAITS

Authentic jerseys with the name of black star athletes on the back, pennants, facial paint (in the home team colors), portable grills for pregame tailgating, and the amazing ability to adapt as personal opinions the pontificating heard on all-sports radio. Members of this species contract a serious illness once a year, diagnosed as "March Madness." The females of this species can be identified by their floral housedresses, Jeff Gordon bedroom slippers, curlers, and bright pink lipstick.

SIMILAR SPECIES

Suburban Sam

Lives outside most cities in a bowling alley called a ranch house. Drives a mini-van and has graduated from penis envy to lawn envy.

Gym Jim

Similar traits to the Weekend Warrior, but without the large stomach. Stays in the gym constantly. Would rather lift a barbell than his wife's skirt.

RANGE

Generally found in cities and towns that support professional, intercollegiate, and high school sports. In other words, like a bad fungus . . . they are practically everywhere. Particularly prevalent in the Northeast, Southeast, Midwest, and the state of Texas during football season.

NATURAL HABITAT

Stadiums, basketball arenas, ACE hardware stores, sports bars, batting cage, miniature golf course, bowling alleys, Saturday morning Little League, under the family car, and in the frozen-food section of the local supermarket.

MATING BEHAVIOR

Copulation usually occurs while holding a television remote during the home team's away games. Sex on a Monday night during the NFL season is considered blasphemous.

CHILD REARING HABITS

Baby given bat and ball in delivery room. Dad explains birds and bees through educational videos supplied by Sportscenter. Baby's first words are "Bud . . . Bud . . . Budweiser."

VACATION SPOTS

Baseball fantasy camps

Baseball Hall of Fame

Puerto Rico and Santa Domingo
for winter baseball

FAVORITE MOVIES

Damn Yankees

Bull Durham

White Men Can't Jump

FAVORITE TELEVISION SHOWS

ESPN Sportscenter
(how did they ever live without it?)

George Michael's Sports Machine
(if they don't have cable)

NBA Showtime with Hannah Storm (they have a sick fantasy involving a deserted island, Hannah Storm, Peter Vescey, and Isiah Thomas as the cute "house boy" with the crossover dribble)

THINGS YOU FIND IN THEIR HOME

NFL and NBA pass to complement
their Direct TV service

Hot dogs, hamburgers, and beer

Horny, frustrated sports widow

SURVIVAL TIPS

Never remind him that he was a waterboy
for the varsity team

Never serve warm beer and cold pizza
during the playoff game

Never, never play with the remote control during
the Ohio State–Michigan game

THE (FRUSTRATED) COMIC

For those white people who have unresolved childhood, emotional, and personal relationship issues but cannot afford to seek professional counseling, there is . . . stand-up comedy. This species is large in number, most drawn to the prospect of being able to turn personal pain into television sitcom success. Patrons of this species are constantly hoping to view a "diamond in the rough," but instead are routinely forced to suffer through an incalculable deluge of dreck . . . with a two-drink minimum.

RECOGNIZABLE TRAITS

Grunge look, spiral notebook, open-mike comedy club passes, antidepressant medication, the *Milton Berle Joke Book,* and a Red Roof Inn travel guide. This species is well versed in explaining why they are "victims" of entertainment politics.

SIMILAR SPECIES

The Crazed Postal Worker

Frustration quotient is similar, but unlike the "broke" comic, this species can afford to buy a gun and shoot their co-workers.

RANGE

Generally found throughout the entire USA with the emergence of comedy club venues. Heavy concentrations in Los Angeles, New York, Boston, Chicago, Seattle, and Disneyland.

NATURAL HABITAT

Comedy clubs, Museum of Broadcasting in NYC (good location for stealing . . . "borrowing" . . . material), cheap diners, college campuses, and the Ed Sullivan Theatre (in the hopes of being spotted by Letterman's people).

MATING BEHAVIOR

Usually with a club waitress, aspiring actress, or a college freshman (after a "killer" show).

CHILD REARING HABITS

Children tend to interfere with upward career movement, and in case the child inherits talent, "Who needs the competition?" Promise to make up for missed time just as soon as they secure a network sitcom.

VACATION SPOTS

None. Vacation is synonymous with unemployment.

FAVORITE MOVIES

King of Comedy

Punchline

Any John Belushi film

FAVORITE TELEVISION SHOWS

Saturday Night Live

The Late Show with David Letterman

The Bugs and Tweety Show

THINGS YOU FIND IN THEIR HOME

The lost episodes of The Honeymooners

The complete Ernie Kovacs retrospective

An empty refrigerator

SURVIVAL TIPS

Never ask this species,

"So, how long are you going to keep
doing this comedy thing?"

SPECIES #5

THE
WASHINGTON
POLITICIAN

n many ways this species considers itself "the chosen ones." Through privileged breeding and an unbearable aura of self-righteousness, these politically well-connected primates are convinced that saving the masses from themselves is their anointed duty. In their world, all who work for them are "yes" men, brownnosers, and faceless bureaucrats who sleep their way to the Lincoln bedroom. The ease with which this species can navigate between ethics, morality, and political expediency is quite astounding. No lie is too big, no bribe too small to reach the prime directive—win at all costs. Better to be in office and under investigation than to be a loser pushing Viagra on television.

RECOGNIZABLE TRAITS

Short haircut, loaded with Vitalis, and reeking of Old Spice, no upper lip, double chin (to match their double-breasted suits), young female "staffer" who moonlights as a mistress, Ben Franklin–style reading glasses (to support the notion that conservatism and intellectualism are synonymous), personalized golf clubs, and the unique ability to talk out of both sides of their mouth. The females can be identified by their Coach briefcase and Nancy Reagan facelift. During congressional recess they can be found in their office making obscene phone calls to Jessie Helms.

SIMILAR SPECIES
Kennedy Liberals

Similar physical features, though they tend to be partial to hair replacement in order to maintain the JFK Camelot look. Glasses are designer horn-rimmed. These liberals are acutely aware of which side of their face looks better on Sunday morning news programs. In the tradition of their idol, they attempt to bed Cokie Roberts and Barbara Walters to get more news coverage.

Political Advisors

Chain smokers, with a "slight" drinking problem. The younger members of this species prefer powder cocaine. High-powered electronic organizers filled with names, numbers, and influential contacts. They always carry the *Washington Post, New York Times,* and the *National Inquirer* (to get the whole story). This species would sell their kids to a Chinese slave ring to get a guest shot on *Imus in the Morning.*

RANGE

Washington-Maryland Beltway, governor's mansions across the USA, and inner-city day-care centers during election years (particularly the South Bronx during presidential elections).

NATURAL HABITAT

Political fundraising dinners, Georgetown, the Yale Club, upscale escort services, and hotel suites that come equipped with a full bar.

MATING BEHAVIOR

Favorite mating call: "Well . . . Barbara Bush swallows!!" Usually married to high school sweetheart. Sex is predicated on political polls. Ultimately, the wife is relegated to political prop in exchange for an unlimited expense account at Neiman Marcus. Please note that sex with a mistress (preferably black or Asian) usually involves spanking.

CHILD REARING HABITS

Other than election years, children are not seen or heard. Children spend the majority of their youth with Mexican nannies until they are old enough to be sent away to private school. Expect all criminal acts to be dismissed through political connections, while parents simultaneously push Capitol Hill for the creation of more prisons.

VACATION SPOTS

Las Vegas (because prostitution is legal)

Amsterdam (because prostitution is legal)

Englewood, N.J. (because that's where Darryl Strawberry lives, and he knows where to find the best prostitutes)

FAVORITE MOVIES

All the President's Men
(considered a training film on how not to get caught)

Citizen Kane
(they nickname their penis "Rosebud")

FAVORITE TELEVISION SHOWS

The McLaughlin Report *(white people tune in to this show because they consider it a sporting event that Puerto Ricans and blacks can't get drafted into)*

Larry King Live *(the only "live" show where the host looks dead)*

After Dark *on the Playboy Channel*

THINGS YOU FIND IN THEIR HOME

Ronald Reagan snot rag

Pat Buchanan's World Domination for Dummies

Autographed picture of Barry Goldwater

A copy of How to Lose Your Nazi Accent, *by Henry Kissinger*

SURVIVAL TIPS

Avoid telling them that strip joints are not tax-deductible.

If visiting the Senate chambers, ask Jesse Helms for the best place to buy southern antiques, hickory barbecue, mammy dolls, and lawn jockeys.

When in Washington, D.C., drop by Teddy Kennedy's office for some Wild Irish Rose Lifesavers.

SPECIES #6

THE CULT
LEADER

For this species, the only thing greater than their ego is their libido. This primate has a direct genetic link to the Wild West snake oil salesman and modern-day used-car dealer. Unlike the Bible Thumper (see page 16), this species has no desire to commercialize Jesus with novelty trinkets (they want the cash direct). Many members of this species do their apprenticeship within the world of professional wrestling, which provides an excellent training ground for learning the fundamentals of mass hypnosis.

RECOGNIZABLE TRAITS

Glazed eyes, bodyguards, a Bible (the one he wrote), Kool-Aid mix, and an American Express Platinum card. There are no female cult leaders . . . except Barbara Walters.

SIMILAR SPECIES

The Con Man

From the same genetic family as the Cult Leader minus the glazed eyes and demon rhetoric. Does not have the ability to have sex and pull off the con at the same time.

RANGE

Western United States. Increasingly seen in the Northwest and parts of San Diego.

NATURAL HABITAT

Desert compounds, Greyhound bus stations, street fairs, and comedy clubs.

MATING BEHAVIOR

Polygamy is a birthright. Has sex with every

woman who believes he is the Savior, the Messiah, and the diaphragm. The species is rumored to be faster than a speeding sperm, able to leap over four bare-breasted women in a single bound, and bend dildos with one hand. However, we have not been able to document this behavior.

CHILD REARING HABITS

Multiple offspring (see mating behavior). Children must take a ticket to give gifts on Father's Day. Children always wear hand-me-downs from victims of cult-induced suicide.

VACATION SPOTS

David Copperfield's trunk (to learn biblical tricks)

Jonesworld (where you can experience virtual reality mass killings)

FAVORITE MOVIES

The Apostle

The Devil's Advocate

The Ten Commandments *(Moses is seen as a role model)*

FAVORITE TELEVISION SHOWS

Home movies made on the compound

THINGS YOU FIND IN THEIR HOME

An FM/AM radio cross

*Children named Jesus Jr., Little Jesus III, JD
Jesus, Jesus of Santa Monica, Big Bubba Jesus,
Bobby Joe, Billy Joe, and Betty Joe Jesus*

SURVIVAL TIPS

None. There are usually no survivors.

THE GEORGIA PEACH

SPECIES #7

There is no species more vain, superficial, self-centered, and clueless than the Georgia Peach. This primate comes from a long line of women whose job it was to put a pretty face on Southern life while looking the other way when their men fathered illegitimate "colored" babies. This modern day Peach has a shelf life of approximately twenty-nine years. She is then replaced by a newer model. This allows her to spend her midlife years knee deep in Southern-fried therapy, Ann Rice novels, and Southern Comfort–flavored Hägen Dazs.

RECOGNIZABLE TRAITS

Big hair, magnolia and mint juleps, long dresses with sorority pens, and a tattoo of Scarlet O'Hara on her big flat ass.

SIMILAR SPECIES

The Southern Gentleman

Has a degree from either Vanderbilt or the University of Virginia. Same stiff mannerisms as the Georgia Peach and still has nightmares from Granddaddy's tales about the Yankees "scorching the family plantation."

RANGE

Southeastern United States.

NATURAL HABITAT

Tours of historic plantations, retired-cheerleader fantasy camps, and sorority dances where the theme song is a rap version of "Dixie."

MATING BEHAVIOR

Prior to mating, this species covers herself with sweet-potato bath oils and a grits facial. Will seek to maintain her virginity until marriage but is most likely to relent to a college football player in the backseat of a Ford. This species has a tendency to confuse "Old Dixie" with "Old Dick."

CHILD REARING HABITS

An overindulgent nature leads to overweight children who bear a striking resemblance to Newt Gingrich. The upbringing for these fat "Baby Newts" will be similar to the children depicted in the movie *The Boys from Brazil.* Hence, they will grow up to be frustrated painters, out-of-work corporals, or *Time* magazine's Man of the Year.

VACATION SPOTS

The Mississippi Governor's Ball

The International Cotton-Pickers Convention

*North Carolina's Miss Tobacco Road
Beauty Pageant*

FAVORITE MOVIES

Gone with the Wind *(a trait shared with the Bible Thumper—see page 16)*

The Little Foxes *(Bette Davis is their kind of bitch)*

Giant *(Rock Hudson is their kind of homosexual)*

FAVORITE TELEVISION SHOWS

Designing Women *(every Southern belle wants to grow up to be Delta Burke)*

Betty Boop *retrospectives on the Cartoon Network*

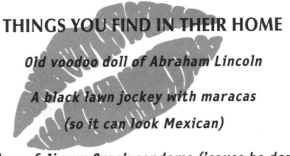

THINGS YOU FIND IN THEIR HOME

Old voodoo doll of Abraham Lincoln

A black lawn jockey with maracas (so it can look Mexican)

A box of Jimmy Crack condoms ('cause he don't care)

SURVIVAL TIPS

Never say to this species, "I wish they all could be California girls."

THE TRAILER TRASH

SPECIES #8

Among the collective that is white people, this species is unique in that they are the most ardent, self-proclaimed believers in the "American Dream" (Mom, apple pie, and the right to shoot first and ask questions later), while reaping the fewest personal rewards. They are dismissed as nothing more than an unfortunate blight by their brethren. Their only useful purpose is at the ballot box and Farm Aid concerts. Every fifty years, one member of this species rises above his or her circumstances and achieves phenomenal financial success (see Ross Perot), thereby providing another half century of hope.

RECOGNIZABLE TRAITS

Dilapidated trailer homes (circa 1975), wheels optional, ZZ Top–style beards for the men, dirt-blond chin hair for the women, plaid shirts, beige Timberlands, and the misplaced belief that no matter how low their station in life, they are still better than any minority, except Michael Jordan.

SIMILAR SPECIES

Poor White Trash

"Kissin' cousin" of Trailer Trash, minus the potential automotive mobility. This species is distinguished by its constant "blood feuds" and love of possum du jour. Usually nests in the Kentucky/Tennessee/West Virginia Appalachian region.

RANGE

Generally found in the Southeast, Midwest, Southwest, and in the rafters at Utah Jazz basketball games.

NATURAL HABITAT

Honky-tonk bars, Beefsteak Charlies (on all-you-can-eat Tuesdays), K-Marts, and evangelical tent revivals.

MATING BEHAVIOR

A fifth of rye, a cheap cigar, and a sixteen-year-old cheerleader are preferable. Masturbation is considered a contact sport.

CHILD REARING HABITS

The more kids, the greater the number of potential government subsidies. Beatings are a form of "bonding," and all boys are required to play football, while never mentioning that they may be "in touch with their feminine side" (cannot handle the suggestion of anything homosexual).

VACATION SPOTS

Loews multiplex movie theaters

Bowling alleys

Any Motel 6 in the state of Florida

FAVORITE MOVIES

Coal Miner's Daughter

Smokey and the Bandit

Debbie Does Dallas

FAVORITE TELEVISION SHOWS

World Wrestling Federation *(especially any pay-per-view event)*

Jerry Springer *(it's the best way to stay in touch with friends and family)*

THINGS YOU FIND IN THEIR HOME (TRAILER)

The complete Jerry Lee Lewis music collection

Hamburger Helper

SURVIVAL TIPS

Never refer to Vietnam as "the war we lost." Never point out that the majority of people on welfare are white. Never request any Motown records on karaoke night.

THE "IN"
NEW YORKER

The mating of '60s idealistic liberals with '80s "greed is good" primates produced this self-centered, proudly dysfunctional, "the world is my oyster" species. Outside of its natural habitat this species is simultaneously condemned and (woefully) imitated by others, all of which serves to produce a feeling of superiority within the species and a natural rivalry with chardonnay-sipping wanna-be Californians.

RECOGNIZABLE TRAITS

First cousin to the Hollywood Executive (see page 102), except wears pinstripe or Ralph Lauren suits, Coach bags, and a Rolex watch. Room-temperature Evian is a must, along with the ability to name-drop with ease. Lives secure in the knowledge that New York City is the center of the universe.

SIMILAR SPECIES

The '60s Greenwich Village Intellectual

Forefather to the "In" New Yorker. While this species was socially conscious, their greatest mistake was adopting a more "liberal" approach to child rearing, which produced a brattish, me-first, culturally devoid generation.

RANGE

Upper Westside, Lower Eastside, and Soho in Manhattan, Los Angeles, Miami, and Aspen, Colorado. Partial to mid-to-large cities.

NATURAL HABITAT

One-bedroom exposed-brick apartments, art galleries, bistro cafés, Starbucks, sushi restaurants, Democratic fundraisers, fashion shows, analyst's couch, and Russell Simmons release parties in the Hamptons. Can be spotted getting off New York City uptown-bound subway before 96th Street.

MATING BEHAVIOR

Stock portfolio serves as an aphrodisiac. Prior to copulation, pops partner's pimples to the sounds of the Artist Formerly Known as Prince. Limousines, airplane bathrooms, and Buddhist temples are favorite breeding grounds. Offspring customarily conceived in late summer in a house share in the Hamptons.

CHILD REARING HABITS

Breastfeeding pump has monogrammed initials. Pampering is considered "concerned parenting." "Time out" replaces firm discipline. First rite of passage is private-school admission.

VACATION SPOTS

Woody Allen's Manhattan (where there are no minorities except blue-black hookers, and everyone lives in gorgeous apartments)

Hilton Head

Any island resort that can impress their co-workers and keep the natives off the compound

FAVORITE MOVIES

Annie Hall

Ghost

Any film that has a weak premise, stilted dialogue, and stars Tom Hanks and Meg Ryan

FAVORITE TELEVISION SHOWS

Seinfeld

Friends

A&E Biography *(they keep expecting to see themselves)*

THINGS YOU FIND IN THEIR HOME

Vintage wine

Any art that dramatizes the color and texture of squash

Black-market tanning lamps

A computer with Internet access (because $19.99 a month to look at sex is cheaper than $100 an hour)

SURVIVAL TIPS

Never tell this species that it's really stupid to spend four dollars for a cup of designer coffee.

THE NATURE NUT

SPECIES #10

This species is determined to "become one with the planet." They refuse to eat meat, buy fur, or wear animal-tested cosmetics (and they hold to the belief that open-toe sandals and wrap-around belts come from the "leather fairy"). Fruit and nuts are treated like M&M's, only organic eggs will do, and water must come out of a bottle from a mountain stream that nobody's ever seen. All of these measures produce, on average, a life expectancy of just two days longer than the rest of the swine-eating, mink-flaunting, Revlon-wearing, chocolate-loving, Pepsi-swilling masses.

RECOGNIZABLE TRAITS

Second-hand bicycle, worn-out Timberlands, acid-rain pamphlets, rice cakes, and a cookbook entitled *One Thousand Ways to Spice Up Your Tofu.*

SIMILAR SPECIES

The Reclusive California Hippie

Replace cookbook with The Doors' greatest hits. This species is susceptible to LSD flashbacks and yearns for the good old days of campus protests, good weed, and free love with nubile virgins.

RANGE

Pacific Northwest, North Dakota, Minnesota, Iowa, and the upper Wyoming region.

NATURAL HABITAT

Log cabins, dense forests, vegetarian markets, Green Peace concerts, and Indian reservations.

MATING BEHAVIOR

Prefers sex in the dirt, under the stars (in order to commune with nature). Can only use condoms made of pig's bladder, in order to protect the ozone layer. To induce hard nipples or firm pecs feed this species wildberries and strained crabgrass juice.

CHILD REARING HABITS

Children are named after plants or seasons (Daisy, Rose, Summer, etc.). Babies are breast fed until the age of five. Any supplemental baby food is made with homegrown ingredients. Greatest fear is that well-meaning neighbors may offer child a Big Mac while babysitting.

VACATION SPOTS

*West Virginia (for the Appalachian
Trail hiking contest)*

*Oregon (for the National Association of Tree
Huggers convention)*

FAVORITE MOVIES

Free Willy

Bambi

*Any film that prominently features talking
animals*

FAVORITE TELEVISION SHOWS

Any Save the Children infomercial (though
they suspect that instead of feeding the children, the food is being eaten by Sally
Struthers's fat ass).

THINGS YOU FIND IN THEIR HOME

Soy burgers

Trail mix

No running water

SURVIVAL TIPS

Never invite this species over for a home-cooked meal consisting of glazed Hawaiian pork, stewed Nigerian oxtails, and hot New York pastrami.

THE
SOUTHERN
(HICK)
FARMER

This species can be found just below the Mason-Dixon Line and slightly above the killer ape on the evolutionary scale. In their glory days this species went by the surname Crow and represented two proof-positive facts of life: one, a little knowledge is a dangerous thing, and two, cousins shouldn't marry. Today, this species maintains a lower profile while exercising substantial regional influence—particularly in the areas of local law enforcement, stock-car racing, and pork rind processing.

RECOGNIZABLE TRAITS

Yellow teeth, deep drawl that belies their eighth-grade education, tractors, and an unnatural relationship with farm animals. The females tend to have more (a) formal education, (b) "colored" friends, and (c) bad-hair days.

SIMILAR SPECIES

The Chicken-Fried Klansman

Unlike the Farmer, this species is smart enough to wear hotel sheets while doing their dirty work but dumb enough to drive their own cars to the scene of the crime.

The Bible Thumper

Smarter than both related species combined and endowed with the unique ability to look you in the face while sticking a knife in your back . . . all in the name of Jesus. See more details about this species on page 16.

RANGE

Below the Mason-Dixon Line (which begins
immediately after the New Jersey Turnpike
on I-95 South).

NATURAL HABITAT

Backwoods moonshining camps, Civil War
reenactments (where the South wins), Big
Boy restaurants, Montgomery Ward, and
baseball card shows.

MATING BEHAVIOR

When it comes to sex, the uglier the better.
Like the Connecticut Yankee, when intoxi-
cated, family members (or young sheep) will
do. Most sexual fantasies involve a black
Amazon female and a trained midget.

CHILD REARING HABITS

Believe in a "hands on" approach to child rearing (child and spousal abuse are considered "inalienable rights") that was "slapped" down from one generation to the next.

VACATION SPOTS

Jefferson Davis's home

Robert E. Lee's home

Sara Lee's home

FAVORITE MOVIES

Driving Miss Daisy *(with the last thirty minutes edited out)*

FAVORITE TELEVISION SHOWS

Roots *(it proves that there was such a thing as a "good" slave owner)*

Country line dancing on TNN

Hee Haw

The Cartoon Network (for "home schooling")

THINGS YOU FIND IN THEIR HOME

An unlimited supply of American-brewed beer

A rope (their motto is "Always be prepared")

Piggly Wiggly coupons

An autographed picture of Yosemite Sam

SURVIVAL TIPS

Never start a joke with "Two black guys walk
into a bar . . ." Remember that for this
species courage comes in numbers, and with
a bottle of "the hard stuff" (preferably
in that order).

THE
COMPUTER
GEEK

SPECIES #12

I n the new revised version of the Bible, edited by Bill Gates, it is written that the geeks shall inherit the earth. In the space of a quarter century this species has gone from the outhouse to the penthouse. Through the wonders of the multibillion-dollar computer technology industry, this species has reached heights of financial success and socially upward mobility that were once considered unattainable. With this success has also come a fundamental personality shift from lovable losers to obnoxious pricks. They are driven to succeed by a burning desire to wreak vengeance on all the jocks, sorority girls, and auto mechanics who made fun of them.

RECOGNIZABLE TRAITS

Scrawny build, which will evolve
into a Joe Couch Potato
physique, reclusive, girl shy, and
able to recite an inordinate
amount of information on violent
computer games and *Gilligan's
Island* trivia. The female geek is
reclusive, possesses a body that's
like a Texas highway—all flat—
and considers cybersex an alter-
native to intercourse.

SIMILAR SPECIES

The Midwest Librarian

Share a connection as the scorned sect of their peers. While shunning computers in favor of the joys of book reading, their free time is spent in preparation for their eventual appearance on *Jeopardy*.

RANGE

Silicon Alley, Silicon Valley, San Francisco Bay Area, the Pacific Northwest, and affluent suburban communities across the Midwest and Northeast.

NATURAL HABITAT

Video arcade parlors, movie
theaters running marathon
Star Wars festivals,
COMP USA outlets, and
Pizza Hut.

MATING BEHAVIOR

Until a financially lucrative position is secured, sticking a hole through a *Hustler* magazine is the primary form of sexual activity. Lovemaking techniques are learned from accessing porno websites.

CHILD REARING HABITS

Since most of their marriages end in divorce, the males are adept at playing weekend father, and the females use Bill Gates as a substitute sibling ("Big Brothcr"). Uses computer graphics for toilet training. Because of their own physical inadequacies, geeks have problems relating to offspring that demonstrate a proclivity for athletics.

VACATION SPOTS

CYBERSPACE

(this way they can avoid as much "human" contact as possible)

COMPUTER CAMP

FAVORITE MOVIES

Star Wars: Episode 1—The Phantom Menace *(to them the computer-animated characters have more depth than the real actors)*

WarGames

2001: A Space Odyssey

FAVORITE TELEVISION SHOWS

Knight Rider *(fantasies about losing virginity in a computer-voice-generated sports car)*

Any Pamela Anderson show

THINGS YOU FIND IN THEIR HOME

Frozen pizza

Extensive comic book collection

Photo collage featuring Bill Gates

SURVIVAL TIPS

Never engage this species in a debate over who was prettier: Ginger, Mary Ann, or Jeannie.

Never refer to a "blow job" as "Steve Job."

Remember, human contact and computer viruses make this species wary, so always recommend "e-mail petting" and "cybersex."

THE GOLDEN
AGE
GAMBLER

For this species, passage into the golden years is the only requisite for the smooth transition from "problem gambler." Usually travels in large groups on rented buses, complete with quiche, tuna sandwiches, and a six-pack of Tab. Fights often break out over ownership of casino coupons. The pressures of career advancement and child rearing have given way to the three truly important elements of life:

1 Being able to find your teeth in the morning

2 Praying that your name will not appear in today's newspaper under the obituary section

3 At all times being in possession of an up-to-date casino bus schedule

RECOGNIZABLE TRAITS

Strong forearms (from years of playing the
one-armed bandit); carries case of Polident,
complete map of Atlantic City and Las Vegas
casinos, and a spare set of Depends
underwear.

SIMILAR SPECIES

The Florida Retiree

Driven by a stronger desire to see their
grandchildren than to gamble. Perfectly con-
tent to work on their gardens and consume
amazing amounts of prune juice. See more
details about this species on page 108.

RANGE

Northeast, Sunbelt, and Palm Springs.

NATURAL HABITAT

Retirement homes, churches, city parks, Atlantic City boardwalk, and any event that's hosted by Willard Scott.

MATING BEHAVIOR

Prior to Viagra, sex was scheduled for four times a year to match the changing seasons. A hot streak at the roulette table can lead to sexual arousal, as can a stiff northwesterly breeze off the Atlantic Ocean. Male fantasies involve giving the high hard one to Vanna White while spinning the Wheel of Fortune. Female fantasies involve making love, doggy style, to Ed McMahon while screaming "You may already be a winner!"

CHILD REARING HABITS

Consider most of their children ungrateful SOBs who can't wait to see them dead—and the feeling is mutual.

VACATION SPOTS

Las Vegas (considered an annual rite of passage)

Any Native American reservation with a casino and a twenty-four-hour all-you-can-eat buffet

FAVORITE MOVIES

Loves movies that show couples sleeping in separate beds, and in which people only come in two colors—black and white

FAVORITE TELEVISION SHOWS

Wheel of Fortune

The Price Is Right

Tae Bo infomercials (because you can't buy porno videos with senior-citizen discount cards)

Nude pictures of Bob Barker

Plastic-covered sofa

A six-month supply of Metamusil

A copy of "How I Beat the Casino"
by One-Eyed Jack

SURVIVAL TIPS

Always remember that, to this species, a good casino is like a good woman . . . liquor in front, poker in the rear.

t is the thankless job of this species to mesh artistic expression, creativity, and imagination with big box-office success, all the while maintaining their place on Hollywood's "A-List"; membership includes priority seating at the best restaurants and a choice of stars to take to the casting couch (remember that's how Wilma made it to Bedrock . . . on her back). This species, often referred to as "suits," takes great pains to ensure that they are never caught on "the road less traveled." There is an understandable link between this species and the Washington Politician (see page 44), inasmuch as both exercise platforms (which include everything from diet to duty) determined by polls and special interests.

RECOGNIZABLE TRAITS

Armani suit, moussed hair, 4 × 4 Range Rover, Ray-Ban sunglasses, carries on intense conversations on a disconnected cell phone ("Will Smith is a fucking genius!!").

SIMILAR SPECIES

The Hollywood Actor

Similar to the Hollywood Executive, but more superficial and with more trips to the plastic surgeon under his belt. The Hollywood Actor spends more money than he makes, to buy things he doesn't need, to impress people he doesn't like.

RANGE

Southern California, film festivals, and parts of downtown Manhattan.

NATURAL HABITAT

Pitch meetings, mud baths at expensive spas, and L.A. Prosecutor's office.

MATING BEHAVIOR

Only occurs standing up (doesn't want to mess up the hair). A mandatory element of the mating ritual: prior to sex, both parties must present an authentic certificate from the American Institute of Silicon and Penal Implants.

CHILD REARING HABITS

Does not raise child according to Dr. Spock, but rather Dr. Strangelove. Insists on Hugo Boss Pampers. Babies do not breast-feed: they only consume champagne and eggs.

VACATION SPOTS

Hawaii

Europe

Heidi Fleiss's apartment

FAVORITE MOVIES

None (if there was a movie they liked, it wouldn't get made)

FAVORITE TELEVISION SHOWS

None (see favorite movies)

THINGS YOU FIND IN THEIR HOME

A complete listing of Hollywood Scientologists (see Cult Leader, page 52)

A family speed-dial directory with relatives listed under: A List (must call); B List (might call), and C List (never call)

A portable casting couch for late night rehearsals

SURVIVAL TIPS

When encountering this species always begin any conversation by saying "I have a three-picture deal . . ."

THE FLORIDA RETIREE

SPECIES #15

This species represents the geriatric version of the American Dream—"Screw the other dumb bastard and live off the interest." A lifetime of scratching and clawing their way to the top of their profession (while avoiding prosecution) is now replaced with thoughts of golf, shuffleboard, and maintaining an inexhaustible supply of Kaopectate. Without this species the makers of cheap hairpieces, white orthopedic shoes, and Oldsmobiles would have to declare bankruptcy. This species was smart enough to take the necessary (financial) measures to avoid their offspring sending them to a refugee camp known as a "senior citizens home."

RECOGNIZABLE TRAITS

Overweight Northerner living in condo-
minium complex. Usually wears XXX-size
flower-printed shirt and white shoes. The
males are never separated from their golf
clubs and carry several bottles of Viagra. The
females wear Greta Garbo sunglasses, orthopedic flip-flops, and ridiculous amounts of
VO5 hairspray.

SIMILAR SPECIES

The Arizona Retiree

Loves the Old West, particularly the near
total genocidal elimination of the American
Indian. Cares much less about Middle East
peace agreements than the Florida Retiree.

RANGE

Central and south Florida.

NATURAL HABITAT

Condo community rooms, sauna, swimming
pool, Disney World, and a bathtub filled with
Bengay.

MATING BEHAVIOR

Copulation usually occurs during a Jackie
Mason comedy routine, but more frequently
manifests itself in a unilateral manner involving Vaseline and a glove. High phone bills
due to a proliferation of calls to 1-900
numbers.

CHILD REARING HABITS

None. Child rearing days finished. Only talk with children once a month because they blame them for wasting their lives.

FAVORITE MOVIES

Cocoon

Cocoon II

The latest Paul Newman, Clint Eastwood, or Jack Nicholson movie (because in them the seventy-year-old gets the girl)

FAVORITE TELEVISION SHOWS

Anything on PBS (didn't you ever wonder who the people were whose "viewer contributions" make the programming possible?)

THINGS YOU FIND IN THEIR HOME

A lifetime supply of Bengay

Keys to a Cadillac

An autographed photograph of Meyer Lansky

SURVIVAL TIPS

NEVER TELL THIS SPECIES TO "ACT YOUR AGE" (THEY MIGHT DROP DEAD).

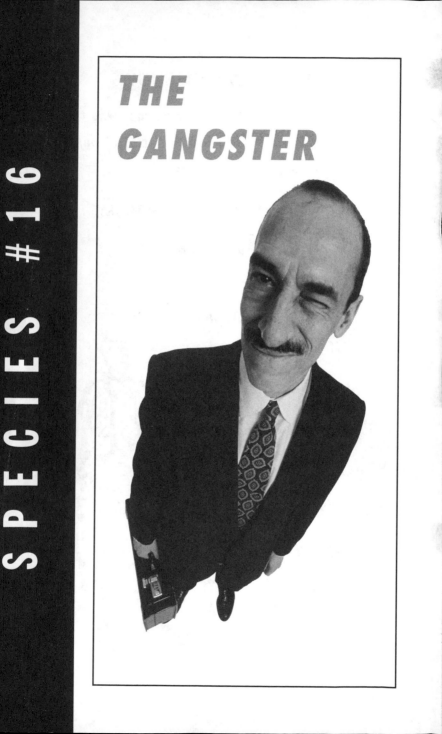

THE
GANGSTER

This species, thanks to extensive media coverage and Hollywood fascination, has reached mythical proportions in North America. Of course, financially lucrative criminal enterprises and a string of corpses from coast to coast have not hurt their image either. This species has demonstrated considerable influence over popular culture, from business ("hostile" takeovers) to hip-hop ("gangster bitches").

RECOGNIZABLE TRAITS

Thousand-dollar suits that look really cheap.
Lawyers, lawyers, and more lawyers. Garlic
lip gloss, and a bumper sticker that reads
"Gangsters Need Love Too." The less pros-
perous members of the species are identified
by their excesses—hair oil and gold chains.
The females are recognizable by their big
hair, fake nails, and incredibly poor taste in
clothing and interior decorating (i.e., expensive homes . . . Wal-Mart furnishings).

SIMILAR SPECIES

None.

RANGE

Entire United States.

NATURAL HABITAT

The trunk of a car with bullet holes, teamster meetings, olive oil conventions, and the backrooms of any "legitimate" nightclub or porn shop.

MATING BEHAVIOR

Copulation is active. The female tends to gain weight after the first offspring (preferably a boy). This species usually has more than one mate—one to have deviant sex with, the other to kiss the children off to school.

CHILD REARING HABITS

First words whispered by baby are "... Whack him." Children usually attend private schools to pick up WASP values and mores. By age six, children learn the difference between tax avoidance and tax aversion. Favorite childhood toy is an ice pick.

VACATION SPOTS

Florida

Cuba (if they could get it back from Castro)

FAVORITE MOVIES

Any film where FBI agents get shot

FAVORITE TELEVISION SHOWS

The Sopranos (gangsters need role models too)

Court TV (this is the equivalent of a comic going on Letterman—you're not really "made" until you stand trial on national television)

THINGS YOU FIND IN THEIR HOME

Large family portraits

Surveillance equipment

SURVIVAL TIPS

If intimately involved with this species, there are only two options:

1 the witness protection program

2 death

THE VALLEY GIRL GROUPIE

SPECIES #17

This species missed the boat when it comes to the ideas of feminism and independent self-determination. "Celebrity boning" is the primary goal of this species. Reading about Leonardo DiCaprio in *The Star* while on line at the grocery store is considered "market research." Never the brightest bulb (regards *Buffy the Vampire Slayer* as a role model), this species was born with stardust in her eyes; and she learned very early how to use all of her *ass-ets* to get ahead.

RECOGNIZABLE TRAITS

High heels, nose job, breast implants, butt implants, and California tan. If employed, will purchase Versace dress to crash celebrity party. Can be spotted the very next day trying to return dress, with semen stain.

SIMILAR SPECIES

The Nonworking Hollywood Actress

Same style as the Valley Girl Groupie, but will initiate sexual quid pro quo. Usually sleeps her way to the middle.

The Hooker

Gets paid more per performance.

RANGE

Los Angeles,
South Beach,
and
Cannes Film
Festival.

MATING BEHAVIOR

If you are a celebrity,
open to all forms of kinky
sex. Will do ménage à trois, whips and
chains, and pull a gerbil out of your ass *if*
your picture does $70 million in domestic
box office. Straight-to-video actors
need not apply.

CHILD REARING HABITS

None. Will not have children.
Refuses to share attention,
gifts, or money with "little
crumb snatchers."

VACATION SPOTS

They do not go on vacation (following celebrities to vacation resorts is work).

FAVORITE MOVIES

How to Marry a Millionaire

FAVORITE TELEVISION SHOWS

Entertainment Tonight

Access Hollywood

Anything on the "E" channel

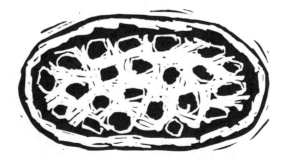

THINGS YOU FIND IN THEIR HOME

Leftover food from a movie set

*Shit-stained boxers stolen from
Brad Pitt's hotel room*

Shoes that are too tight for her feet

SURVIVAL TIPS

When considering intercourse with this
promiscuous species, use two condoms and
aluminum foil. It may not prevent disease,
but it will clear up the reception
on your television.

SPECIES #18

THE SURVIVALIST

This species takes their cue from the motto *"Inside every flag-waving patriot is a gun-toting, Aryan nation–subscribing, neo-Nazi-sympathizing, tax-evading nut."* The Survivalist has no time for bleeding-heart liberals (unless they are responsible for the bleeding) or foot-dragging conservatives, yet they have no problem accepting government-issued greenbacks (tax refunds) to finance their call to arms. This species is among the first to say that if others have a problem with this country they should "go back to wherever they came from"; yet when the Survivalist feels he has been treated unjustly, he is willing to pack up and go no farther north than Montana.

RECOGNIZABLE TRAITS

Army fatigues, NRA bus pass, a subscription to *House & Garden Gun Range,* wallet-size pictures of the Federal Building in Oklahoma, and army surplus bulletproof condoms . . . and that's the females. The males are recognized by their crewcuts, handguns, and genetically deformed testicles.

SIMILAR SPECIES

The Militiaman

A weekend Survivalist. Cannot do it full-time because of his job, usually at a county waste station. Dreams of leaving his family and starting a used-gun business.

RANGE

Entire United States, but heavy nesting occurs in the Midwest and West.

NATURAL HABITAT

Gun fairs, gas station repair shops, and a picnic at Charlton Heston's house.

MATING BEHAVIOR

When it comes to copulation, the Survivalist motto is *"Happiness is a warm gun."* Constant mating is a staple of this species. Motivation is to stave off white people needing quotas and affirmative action by the year 2050.

CHILD REARING HABITS

Baby wears Kevlar diapers. Only allows children to view television programs and websites that are extremely violent and promote the overthrow of the government. To promote early childhood education, takes children to paint-ball war games.

VACATION SPOTS

Waco, Texas

*Any city or state where the minority population
is less than 1 percent (and the city of Boston)*

FAVORITE MOVIES

Conspiracy

Police Academy 1–4

Natural Born Killers

FAVORITE TELEVISION SHOWS

None (they're waiting for "The Gun Channel")

THINGS YOU FIND IN THEIR HOME

Propane, wires, and fertilizers

David Koresh's portrait

Loose stools (because they don't give a shit)

The Field Guide to White People

SURVIVAL TIPS

When in the company of this species, never say "I think the government is doing a fine job."

Never volunteer to drive the fertilizer truck to the state fair.

WHITE PEOPLE'S GOLDEN RULES

Never make a racial comment among friends unless you know everyone's lineage.

For the white business owner, always hire a black Hispanic woman. This way you can report that you've hired three minorities (if you're lucky, she will also be handicapped).

Never ask a person of Asian descent for directions to a Chinese or Japanese restaurant.

Always emphasize your intellectual and educational achievements among minorities. This will compensate for the overwhelming sense of physical inferiority that many white people have.

Play dumb if someone asks you why there were no blacks on the Titanic.

If a Latino family moves next door to you, do not ask them if they can teach you the Macarena.

Try ethnic dining once a week. This will allow you to travel the globe while passing gas at home.

Promote the X-treme Games. It's one of the few sports where white people are actually the stars.

Only vacation in Europe, Canada, or Australia. These rules apply there.

Things WHITE PEOPLE TAKE CREDIT FOR

The Slam Dunk

Jazz

Rock 'n' Roll

Little Richard

Gunpowder

KENTUCKY FRIED CHICKEN

SEX

(Doggy-Style)

SLANG

Cleopatra

SWING DANCING

THE UNDERGROUND RAILROAD

Salsa

Spaghetti

Def Comedy Jam

The Tan

The Street Light

The Pyramids

THE COTTON GIN

COOL

Things WHITE PEOPLE SHOULD TAKE CREDIT FOR

 *Colonization*

JEFFREY DAHMER,

*who promoted the concept of
eating black people with hot sauce*

The Middle
Passage

MASS WARFARE
ON A GLOBAL SCALE

A STARBUCKS ON EVERY CORNER IN NEW YORK CITY

Feeding Al Roker donuts in the morning

Breastfeeding in public with a tattooed nipple

No black Friends on Friends

CASTING

ITALIAN ACTORS

IN LATIN FILMS

Not washing their hands after using the bathroom

He had to give himself a beating as a child because his parents were afraid it would lower his self-esteem.

The only food in her refrigerator is a bottle of water and a cup of yogurt.

He has a one-day tan and it's December.

He believes that impotence is a birthright, not a medical condition.

She believes breast implants are a birthright, not a surgical procedure.

He believes therapy is a hobby.

He's chosen to be the owner when kids pick sides for a basketball game.

She puts the housekeeper and babysitter as references on her resume.

He thanks his lawyer and accountant instead of God at an awards show.

She believes dinner at Taco Bell is ethnic dining.

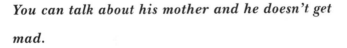

You can talk about his mother and he doesn't get mad.

He refers to black athletes as "thoroughbreds" and "greyhounds" and white athletes as "heady" and "gritty."

...built for basketball...

About the Authors

Stephan Dweck has worked as a prominent entertainment attorney specializing in music, film, and television. His clients included over forty recording artists ranging from current top-forty bands on major labels to underground acts that he cultivated. Stephan also represented over seventy-five currently working television and film actors. He was the co-executive producer for the HBO *Snaps* specials. Stephan sits on the Law Advisory Board for Quinnipiac College School of Law.

Monteria Ivey is a comedian/author/actor/screenwriter. Monteria was the co-executive producer and host for the HBO *Snaps* television specials. He was the host of *Think Twice,* the first adult game show produced for PBS. He is affiliated with the Black Filmmaker Foundation and works regularly for HBO on their stand-up comedy specials as well as the annual HBO/Toyota Comedy Festival held in New York City. Monteria is currently working on HBO's *The Chris Rock Show.*

Together they are the authors of the best-selling books on African-American humor entitled *Snaps, Double Snaps,* and *Triple Snaps* (William Morrow). Their latest books are *You're So Fine I'd Drink A Tub Of Your Bath Water*, and *Baby, All Those Curves and Me With No Brakes* (Hyperion-Disney). They have worked with such talent as Quincy Jones, Wesley Snipes, Chris Rock, Martin Lawrence, George Carlin, Queen Latifah, LL Cool J, Veronica Webb, Dana Carvey, Alan King, Ray Romano, Mark Curry, Ice-T, Tommy Davidson, Heavy D, Paul Mooney, and Coolio, just to name a few.

Ivey & Dweck have written screenplays for Paramount Pictures and Miramax Films. Their latest screenplay is entitled *The Field Guide to White People*, slated to go into production in November 1999.

Ivey & Dweck have been the subject of articles for the *New York Times*, the *Wall Street Journal*, the *Washington Post*, the *Los Angeles Times*, the *Philadelphia Inquirer*, *USA Today*, *Vanity Fair*, *Newsweek*, *People*, and *Entertainment Weekly*. They have appeared on *Imus in the Morning* (MSNBC), the *Tom Snyder Show* (CNBC), *Charlie Rose* (PBS), *CNN*, *CBS News*, *Fox News*, *UPN News*, *American Journal*, the *Tom Joyner Morning Show*, the *Donnie Simpson Radio Show*—WPGC, and the *Howard Stern Show*.